Grades 2–4

MORE ADVENTURES OF THE DETECTIVE CLUB

MYSTERIES FOR YOUNG THINKERS

JUDY LEIMBACH
AND SHARON ECKERT

Routledge
Taylor & Francis Group
NEW YORK AND LONDON

First published 2007 by Prufrock Press Inc.

Published in 2021 by Routledge
605 Third Avenue, New York, NY 10017
2 Park Square, Milton Park, Abingdon, Oxon OX14 4RN

Routledge is an imprint of the Taylor & Francis Group, an informa business

Edited by Lacy Elwood
Editorial Assistant: Kate Sepanski
Illustrated by Mike Eustis
Production Design by Marjorie Parker

ISBN 13: 978-1-59363-222-9 (pbk)

Contents

Teacher's Guide: Introduction

In our previous book, *Detective Club: Mysteries for Young Thinkers*, students enjoyed joining the Detective Club and working along with the young detectives as they solved the mysteries. In *More Adventures of the Detective Club*, young students will enjoy the challenge of solving four new mysteries while developing their thinking skills. Students will learn to think critically and to employ problem-solving strategies. This book will help develop a variety of skills encouraged by national standards in each discipline of study.

While solving the mysteries in this book, students will gather clues through:
* using inferential thinking,
* solving logic puzzles,
* sorting information,
* solving word puzzles, and
* decoding messages.

In order to reach the correct conclusions, students will use the following skills:
* analyzing clues,
* organizing information,
* combining and analyzing the information,
* using deductive reasoning, and
* using the process of elimination.

The teacher will be able to assess the students' skill level in the above areas by observing the way they approach a problem and apply the skills to draw conclusions. Evaluation of student performance will be based on those observations, as well as on the students' success in reaching the correct answers. Other important areas of assessment include the student's ability to work with others if working with a partner or group, growth in his or her level of independence in working puzzles on his or her own, and perseverance demonstrated as he or she meets the challenges presented in each mystery.

In this book, Shirley Sharp, the main character in *Detective Club*, has moved to a new city, misses her old Detective Club friends, and decides to start a new club. She advertises for members and creates a series of tests for membership in the club. The first part of the book, "Shirley's Tests for New Members," introduces students to some types of puzzles they will need to do in order to solve the mysteries in the book. When students have demonstrated their understanding of the various types of puzzles by successfully completing Shirley's tests, they become members of the Detective Club and are ready to work along with the detectives solving the cases in the book.

The four mysteries in this book are longer and more challenging than those in the first *Detective Club* book. Each mystery includes a separate teacher's guide with instructions for the teacher and the answers to the puzzles.

Solving the Puzzles on Shirley's Tests

This introductory section gives students the opportunity to work the puzzles applicants for membership into the Detective Club will be required to solve. There are four matrix logic puzzles, an anagram puzzle, and two cryptograms.

If students have not had previous experience solving matrix logic puzzles, it is suggested that you work through some of these together as they learn to record the information gained from the clues and use the grid to help them reach their conclusions. Be sure the students understand that whenever they use a matrix to solve a logic puzzle:
* A "no" is as important as a "yes" in reaching conclusions.
* Every time they fill in a "yes," they need to fill in the grid with "nos" both horizontally and vertically.

See the Teacher's Guide pages at the end of the "Shirley's Tests" section for more information.

When students have completed all of the puzzles on Shirley's Tests, they can be given their certificates of membership and identification cards. They can then move on to work through the mysteries with Shirley and the other members of the Detective Club.

Solving the Detective Club Mysteries

The first mystery in the book is the easiest, so it is a good place to start after students have solved the puzzles in Shirley's Tests. You may work through some of the puzzles with the class, have them work with partners, or allow them to work independently, depending on their grade level and the level of success students had with puzzles of each type included in Shirley's Tests. After successfully completing the first mystery in the book, it is not necessary to do the others in any particular sequence.

The Case of the Missing Prize

Students first solve a matrix logic puzzle to determine which prizes were won by five of the pupils in Mrs. Brady's class. Shirley's little sister, Sara, enlists the help of the Detective Club when her classmate's first-place medal disappears from his desk while the class is attending a party in the school library. Sara and the other students in Mrs. Brady's class are dressed as storybook characters for the party. To find the suspects, students must solve logic puzzles to determine what costume each student is wearing. To decide who is the most likely suspect, students will analyze the information the detectives gather when they question the six characters who were observed entering or leaving the classroom during the party.

The Case of the Lost Charm Bracelet

Shirley and Betty find a silver charm bracelet in the locker room after their swimming lessons at the Fairfield Park District where Betty's mother works. To find the owner of the charm bracelet, students must collect information and record it on a chart that will lead them to the correct conclusion. Information is gathered by analyzing class lists, solving a matrix logic puzzle, making inferences, and drawing conclusions from enrollment cards, data received from counselors, and students' vacation postcards.

The Case of the Missing Mascot

Cory's older sister, Carrie, and the other Fairfield North cheerleaders discover their Tommy Tiger mascot costume is missing. The cheerleaders from their rival team have taken it, and hidden a series of clues they must follow to find Tommy Tiger. Cory offers the services of the Detective Club to help solve the puzzle clues. To solve the case, students will need to break a code and decode a message, solve a variety of number puzzles, use the process of elimination to reach conclusions, use matrix logic puzzles to find addresses of the cheerleaders and the Fairfield South starting players, and use the last clues to determine the location where they will find the Tommy Tiger mascot costume.

The Treasure Hunt

Cory and Bill offer to help their teacher plan a class party by creating puzzle clues for a Treasure Hunt. They enlist the aid of the other Detective Club members. To locate the treasure, students will have to use some reference materials and the given clues to identify a particular United States president, break the code of a cryptogram puzzle, unscramble the letters to interpret an anagram clue, complete a logic matrix puzzle, and solve a number puzzle that will give them the room number where the treasure will be found.

SHIRLEY'S TESTS FOR NEW MEMBERS

Shirley's Detective Agency

Shirley's Tests for New Members
Starting Over: The New Detective Club

Hi, I'm Shirley Sharp. Maybe some of you have met me before. My friends, Rita Right, Quent Quick, Sam Smart, and I were members of a Detective Club back in my old hometown. We had lots of fun together helping people in our neighborhood solve mysteries. We were good at finding missing things, like a lost wallet and a missing prize. Once, we even tracked down a missing birthday cake.

Now my family has moved into an apartment complex in a new town, Fairfield, and I really miss the old Detective Club. I miss my old friends, and I really miss the challenge of solving mysteries. I liked the excitement of pondering clues, working through puzzles, and finding solutions.

So, I have decided to start up a new Detective Club here in Fairfield. Because I'm new in town, I don't really know which kids are really good thinkers and enjoy puzzles as much as I do.

I decided to advertise for possible members. I made a sign to put up in our apartment complex, and I made up a series of tests to check out who would be a good member for my club. Anyone who is interested in joining the club will have to pass the tests. They are some hard tests, but detective work isn't easy!

I waited anxiously for kids to apply to join my club. The first two who came to see me were not

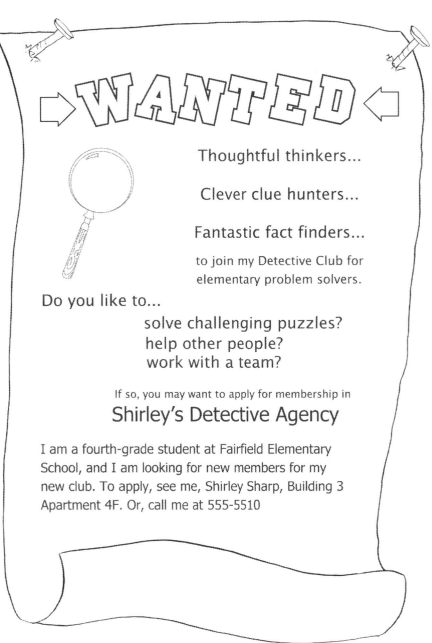

WANTED

Thoughtful thinkers...

Clever clue hunters...

Fantastic fact finders...

to join my Detective Club for elementary problem solvers.

Do you like to...

solve challenging puzzles?
help other people?
work with a team?

If so, you may want to apply for membership in

Shirley's Detective Agency

I am a fourth-grade student at Fairfield Elementary School, and I am looking for new members for my new club. To apply, see me, Shirley Sharp, Building 3 Apartment 4F. Or, call me at 555-5510

really serious puzzle solvers. They took one look at the puzzles on my tests for new members and left without even trying!

The next two were brother and sister, Bill and Betty Bright. They both dived right into the puzzles, and raced each other to see who could complete them first. They were so excited when I told them they passed the tests and gave them their official Detective Club Identification Cards.

The next day, they brought their friend, Cory Quest, who they knew loved puzzles. Sure enough, he enjoyed the challenge, easily passed the test, and happily became the fourth member of the Detective Club.

You can become a member too. Solve the series of puzzles on my new member tests and earn your certificate of membership and Detective Club ID. Then you can work right along with the club members, solving the puzzles each mystery presents. Good luck!

Shirley's Tests for New Members
Finding Ages

Test 1 is the easiest of the seven tests. It is a warm-up exercise for your brain.

Directions: The two clues below will help you find out the correct ages for Jody, Luke, Katie, and Jorge.

Hint: The first clue does not tell you Luke's age, but it does tell you two ages he cannot be. In solving logic puzzles, always remember that the "no" clues are very important.

Clues

1. Luke's age is not an even number.
2. Katie, whose age is an even number, is older than Jody, but younger than Luke.

Ages	7	8	9	10
Jody				
Luke				
Katie				
Jorge				

Shirley's Tests for New Members
Good Sports

Jim, Joe, John, Jeff, and Jake are all good sports. However, each is only really good at playing one sport. Using the three clues below, you should easily be able to find the sport at which each boy excels.

Good Sports	Baseball	Soccer	Tennis	Football	Skating
Jim					
Joe					
John					
Jeff					
Jake					

Clues
1. Jake's ability to throw a ball makes him good in his sport.
2. Jim, John, and Jake use a round ball in their sports.
3. Joe and the skater watched John's soccer game.

Name:_____ Date:_____

Shirley's Tests for New Members
Favorite Desserts

Favorite Desserts	Chocolate Chip Cookies	Apple Pie	Chocolate Cake	Butter Pecan Ice Cream	Chocolate Fudge Ice Cream	Strawberry Shortcake
Rahul						
Molly						
Kenny						
Michael						
Brenda						
Eric						

This test might make you hungry! This time you have to match Rahul, Molly, Kenny, Michael, Brenda, and Eric with their favorite yummy desserts.

Clues
1. Kenny's favorite dessert has fruit in it, but Michael's does not.
2. Eric's favorite dessert has chocolate in it.
3. The two girls must store their favorite dessert in the freezer.
4. Eric and the boy who loves chocolate cake play ball with Rahul and the pie lover.
5. Rahul and Molly are allergic to chocolate.

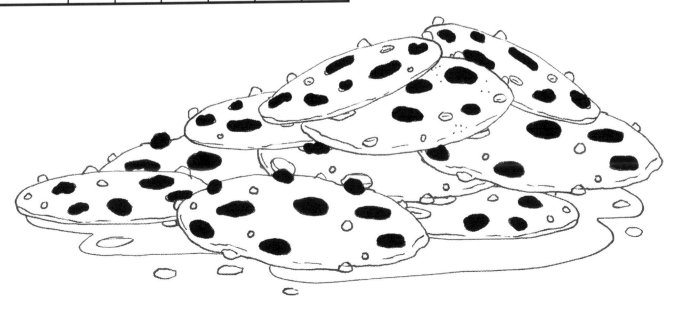

Shirley's Tests for New Members
Anagram Puzzle

This is a different kind of puzzle, called an anagram. In an anagram puzzle, all of the correct letters are in each word, but they are scrambled. For example: the word "HAPPY" might be written as "YPHPA" and "SAD" as "DSA."

Put on your thinking cap and unscramble the letters in the anagram puzzle below:

D O G O   T E C T E D S E V I   E A R   O D O G

_____   _____   _____   _____

K N H T I E S R   O H W   E U S

_____   _____   _____

E U S L C   O T

_____   _____

V O L S E   Z U L P Z S E.

_____   _____.

Shirley's Tests for New Members
Cryptogram Puzzle

Cryptogram puzzles are another type of challenging word game. In a cryptogram puzzle, each letter stands for some other letter. There is no alphabetical pattern. A letter may represent any other letter, but it stays the same through the whole puzzle. For example, if M = S; L = H; O = I; B = R; G = L; A = E; P = Y; and C = T, then Shirley's Tests would be written as **MLOBGAP'M CAMCM**.

Try the cryptogram puzzle below. The words in the list are all fruits. To make it a little easier, the vowels all represent another vowel, and the consonants represent another consonant. *Hint*: Begin by solving the first five letter puzzle. Look at the double letters and think about a fruit with a double letter in its name.

I D D J O   D O I N S

___ ___ ___ ___ ___   ___ ___ ___ ___ ___

N I B M I J A E D O

___ ___ ___ ___ ___ ___ ___ ___ ___ ___

C I M O Z P O J A B

___ ___ ___ ___ ___ ___ ___ ___ ___ ___

Shirley's Tests for New Members
Cryptogram Riddle

In the cryptogram riddle below, each consonant represents another consonant, and each vowel represents another vowel. Begin by looking for one-letter words, double letters, and punctuation marks like apostrophes and question marks. These can be helpful clues in guessing what the letters stand for and what the puzzle says. *Hint*: In this puzzle, the consonant N represents the consonant B, the consonant S represents the consonant R, and the vowel U represents the vowel O.

Riddle:

R L O D   M U   W U I   P O C C O

____ ____ ____ ____ ____ ____ ____ ____ ____ ____ ____ ____ ____ ____

Z O B G E S A ' J   J U T ?

____ ____ ____ ____ ____ ____ ' ____   ____ ____ ____ ?

Answer:

O   N O D   N U W

____   ____ ____ ____   ____ ____ ____

Shirley's Tests for New Members
Pen Pals

Connor, Megan, Anji, Bryan, Lindsay, Matt, and Annie are sixth graders who have pen pals they have been writing to since third grade. Each of their pen pals lives in a different state. Follow the clues to the state where each one of their pen pals lives.

Pen Pals	Colorado	Alaska	New Mexico	Alabama	Florida	New York	Rhode Island
Connor							
Megan							
Anji							
Bryan							
Lindsay							
Matt							
Annie							

Clues
1. Connor, Bryan, and Matt write to friends that live in states that have two words in their names.
2. Annie and Anji write to pen pals who live in states that begin with the same letter as their own first names.
3. Lindsay, Bryan, and Matt all write to friends who live east of the Mississippi River.
4. Neither Connor nor Anji send letters to the largest or smallest state, but Annie and Matt do.

Detective Club Certificate of Membership

This certifies that _____ has passed the challenging new member tests and is now an official member of the Detective Club.

Congratulations from Shirley Sharp, Detective Club President

Shirley Sharp

Detective Club Certificate of Membership

This certifies that _____ has passed the challenging new member tests and is now an official member of the Detective Club.

Congratulations from Shirley Sharp, Detective Club President

Shirley Sharp

Detective Club
Official Identification Card

Name _____

Shirley Sharp

Detective Club President

Date Issued _____

Detective Club
Official Identification Card

Name _____

Shirley Sharp

Detective Club President

Date Issued _____

Detective Club
Official Identification Card

Name _____

Shirley Sharp

Detective Club President

Date Issued _____

Detective Club
Official Identification Card

Name _____

Shirley Sharp

Detective Club President

Date Issued _____

Detective Club
Official Identification Card

Name _____

Shirley Sharp

Detective Club President

Date Issued _____

Detective Club
Official Identification Card

Name _____

Shirley Sharp

Detective Club President

Date Issued _____

Detective Club
Official Identification Card

Name _____

Shirley Sharp

Detective Club President

Date Issued _____

Detective Club
Official Identification Card

Name _____

Shirley Sharp

Detective Club President

Date Issued _____

Detective Club
Official Identification Card

Name _____

Shirley Sharp

Detective Club President

Date Issued _____

Detective Club
Official Identification Card

Name _____

Shirley Sharp

Detective Club President

Date Issued _____

Shirley's Tests for New Members
Teacher's Guide

Finding Ages (p. 9)

If students have not had experience with using a matrix to solve logic puzzles, you may want to lead them through the steps of this first puzzle:
1. Clue 1 tells them Luke is not 8 or 10. Mark "no" or "X" in those spaces.
2. Clue 2 tells them Katie is not 7 or 9. Mark "no" or "X" in those spaces.
3. If Katie is older than Jody, Jody cannot be 10. Mark a "no" or "X" in that space.
4. If Katie is younger than Luke, Katie cannot be 10. Mark a "no" or "X" in that space. Therefore, Katie is 8. Mark "yes" or "O" to mark that spot, and "no" or "X" for the others who are not 8. This leads to the conclusion that Jorge is 10. Mark "yes" or "O" in that space and "no" or "X" that Jorge is not 7 or 9.
5. Students can now see that Jody and Luke are the 7 and 9 year olds. If Katie is older than Jody and younger than Luke, Jody is 7 and Luke is 9.

Answers: Jody is 7; Luke is 9; Katie is 8; and Jorge is 10.

Good Sports (p. 10)

If students need help, the following information can be gained from the clues:
1. "Throwing" is not an important skill in soccer, tennis, or skating, therefore "no" can be placed in those spaces for Jake.
2. Jim, John, and Jake do not ice skate or play football.
3. Neither Joe nor John can be the skater. John plays soccer.

Answers: Jim plays tennis; Joe plays football; John plays soccer; Jeff is the skater; and Jake plays baseball.

Favorite Desserts (p. 11)

Clues can be interpreted in the following way:
1. Kenny's favorite dessert is either apple pie or strawberry shortcake, but Michael's is neither of those.
2. Eric's favorite is one of the three desserts with "chocolate" in its name.

3. The two girls' favorites are the ice creams; therefore none of the boys has ice cream for his favorite dessert.
4. Neither Eric nor Rahul are the boy who loves chocolate cake or apple pie.
5. Rahul and Molly's favorite desserts are not any of the three desserts with chocolate.

Answers: Rahul likes strawberry shortcake; Molly likes butter pecan ice cream; Kenny likes apple pie; Michael likes chocolate cake; Brenda likes chocolate ice cream; and Eric likes chocolate chip cookies.

Anagram Puzzle (p. 12)

If students are unfamiliar with anagrams, explain that in an anagram puzzle all of the correct letters are there, but the words are scrambled. In addition to the two examples given on the puzzle page, you may want to do some more practice words with the class. An easy way to demonstrate anagrams is to have each student write his or her name with the letters scrambled.

Answer: Good detectives are good thinkers who use clues to solve puzzles.

Cryptogram Puzzle (p. 13)

Explain that each letter in a cryptogram puzzle stands for some other letter. There is no pattern, such as each letter representing the letter that comes before or after it in the alphabet. The letters randomly represent another letter, but each letter consistently represents the same thing throughout a particular puzzle. To make it a little easier, consonants represent consonants and vowels represent vowels. Have students solve the apple puzzle first, instructing them to think about a fruit with double letters in its name.

Answers: apple; peach; cantaloupe; watermelon

Cryptogram Riddle (p. 14)

Read over the directions with the students and direct them to begin by filling in the letters given in the hint: B, R, and O. You may want to point out that the sentence ends with a question mark, and that one of the words has an apostrophe in it. Remind students that consonants represent consonants and vowels represent vowels.

Riddle: What do you call a vampire's son?
Answer: A bat boy.

Pen Pals (p. 15)

For any students who continue to need help with the clues to solve logic puzzles:

1. Connor, Bryan, and Matt do not write to friends in Colorado, Alaska, or Florida.
2. Annie and Anji don't write to friends in Colorado, New Mexico, Florida, New York, or Rhode Island. Because Annie and Anji write to the two people in Alaska and Alabama, none of the other students do.
3. Lindsay, Bryan, and Matt do not write to friends in Colorado, Alaska, or New Mexico.
4. Annie and Matt write to friends in either Alaska or Rhode Island; none of the others do.

Answers: Connor writes to New Mexico; Megan writes to Colorado; Anji writes to Alabama; Bryan writes to New York; Lindsay writes to Florida; Matt writes to Rhode Island; and Annie writes to Alaska.

Certificates and Identification Cards

Award the students the Detective Club Certificates of Membership and Official Identification Cards on pp. 16–17 after they have successfully solved the puzzles. If possible, laminate the Identification Cards for the students.

THE CASE OF THE MISSING MEDAL

Shirley's Detective Agency

The Case of the Missing Medal
Sara and the Summer Reading Club Winners

When school started in the fall, Shirley Sharp's little sister, Sara, was happy to be in Mrs. Brady's second-grade class. She had heard from other kids that Mrs. Brady was a nice teacher who liked to make up puzzles for her students.

Sara, like her older sister, loved solving puzzles. She also liked to read and had read many books over the summer as a member of the public library's Summer Reading Club. The first week of school, Mrs. Brady announced the names of the five students in her class who had read the most books in the Summer Reading Club. Sara was proud to be one of them!

Then, true to her reputation, Mrs. Brady gave the class a puzzle she made up to find out which prize each of the five winning students had won. Sara, being a puzzle whiz, easily solved the puzzle using the clues and grid below. *Hint*: Remember that the student who placed first is the student who read the most books.

Prize Winners	1st	2nd	3rd	4th	5th
Jacob					
Dominic					
Tenille					
Sara					
Patricia					

Clues
1. Tenille and the boy who placed third read fewer books than Dominic.
2. Patricia read more books than Sara, but fewer than Dominic and Tenille.

The Case of the Missing Medal
The Costume Party

The school library at Fairfield Elementary School had been remodeled over the summer, and Ms. Riggs, the school librarian, invited all of the classes to attend a party to dedicate the new library. The prizes for the Summer Reading Club would be given out in each class before the party.

Mrs. Brady asked the children in her class if they would like to dress up as storybook characters for the school library dedication party. They all thought that would be lots of fun.

The homework for the next day in Sara's class was to turn in forms that would tell Mrs. Brady what characters they would be. They were to keep it a secret, because Mrs. Brady was planning to make character puzzles for the other classes to solve the day of the party.

The morning of the party, all of the children in Sara's class were excited as they arrived in their costumes. They had fun guessing each other's characters. Before they left their classroom, Mrs. Brady gave Sara, Patricia, Jacob, Tenille, and Dominic their prizes for the Summer Reading Club. They each received a certificate, a bookmark, and a pencil that said "Super Reader." Dominic also got a gold medal on a ribbon to wear around his neck, like an Olympic champion!

When it was time to go to the party, Dominic removed his medal and placed it in his desk. Mrs. Brady asked him why he wasn't wearing his medal.

He replied, "Well, it really doesn't go with my costume."

She laughed and said, "I guess you're right about that!"

The party in the library was lots of fun. There were stories and songs and games and treats, and Ms. Riggs had Sara's class parade around the library in their storybook character costumes so everyone could admire them.

When the party ended, everyone returned to their classrooms to get ready for lunch. The first thing Dominic wanted to do was put his medal back on so he could wear it to the lunchroom. But, when he opened his desk, he couldn't find the medal. It had disappeared!

As the other children left for lunch, Mrs. Brady came over to help him check his desk, but it was not there. It was gone.

Sara Sharp was waiting for Dominic in the lunchroom.

"My sister, Shirley, and her friends are great detectives," she told him. "Maybe they can find your missing medal."

When the detectives heard Dominic's story, they used their lunch hour to work on the case. Billy Bright had the first idea. "There were teachers in the hall during the dedication party. Let's check with whoever was in the hall by the second-grade classrooms."

"Mrs. Mills was in the hallway by our classroom," said Sara.

When they talked to Mrs. Mills, she said she had seen some characters go in Mrs. Brady's room during the party. Shirley Sharp pulled out her detective notebook and asked, "Can you tell us which characters you saw?"

"Let me think," Mrs. Mills replied. "I saw Little Red Riding Hood and Clifford go in and come out together. Soon after that I saw Peter Rabbit. After he came out, Curious George went in. I remember seeing someone dressed as the Big Bad Wolf walk in with someone dressed like a little pig. The wolf came out first, and I wondered what happened to the little pig. But, it came out a couple minutes later."

"OK," said Shirley. "Our next step is to get Mrs. Brady's four costume puzzles that were handed out at the party and figure out who was wearing what costume. Then we will have our list of suspects."

Each of the detectives solved one of the puzzles, and they had their six suspects in a flash. Can you solve the puzzles and find out who the suspects are?

The Case of the Missing Medal
Costume Party Puzzle 1

Find the correct costume for each of the four girls and two boys in this puzzle.

Clues
1. None of the girls plans to dress as a boy or as an animal.
2. Patricia and Brendan will dress as brother and sister, and Jane will come as their friend.
3. Andrew and Laura's costumes will definitely be red.

Storybook Characters	Arthur	D. W.	Francine	Clifford	Goldilocks	Little Red Riding Hood
Laura						
Patricia						
Andrew						
Brendan						
Jane						
Tenille						

The Case of the Missing Medal
Costume Party Puzzle 2

Find the correct costume for each of the three girls and three boys in this puzzle.

Clues

1. Douglas and Miguel will dress as animals.

2. Elizabeth and Douglas are older than their classmates who will be Amelia Bedelia and Peter Rabbit.

3. The boy who will be Nate the Great walks to school with Elizabeth, Hannah, and the girl who will be Cinderella.

Storybook Characters	Curious George	Miss Frizzle	Peter Rabbit	Cinderella	Amelia Bedelia	Nate the Great
Douglas						
Hannah						
Mary						
Daniel						
Elizabeth						
Miguel						

The Case of the Missing Medal
Costume Party Puzzle 3

Find the correct costume for each of the three girls and three boys in this puzzle.

Clues

1. None of the three boys wanted to be Snow White, and none of the girls wanted to be the Little Pig.
2. Sara and Dominic are the only ones who have same first initial as their character.
3. Tayshawn's character has a name that is the opposite of Hailey's.
4. Jacob, Katherine, and the girl who was Snow White are good friends.

Storybook Characters	Snow White	Grumpy	Happy	Dopey	Sneezy	Little Pig
Tayshawn						
Dominic						
Hailey						
Katherine						
Jacob						
Sara						

The Case of the Missing Medal
Costume Party Puzzle 4

Find the correct costume for each of the three girls and three boys in this puzzle.

Clues

1. Stephanie and Choya will dress as Dr. Seuss characters.
2. The name of Brett's character contains all of the letters found in his first name.
3. Stephanie and Juan are shorter than the boy who will be Harry Potter, but taller than the girls who will be the Wicked Witch and the Cat in the Hat.

Storybook Characters	The Grinch	Big Bad Wolf	Cat in the Hat	Berenstain Bear	Harry Potter	Wicked Witch
Zachary						
Stephanie						
Juan						
Choya						
Janelle						
Brett						

The Case of the Missing Medal
Cracking the Case

Shirley took out the six pages in her detective notebook where she had written the six suspects, one costume on each page. "We will need to question each of these six students," she told the others. "Betty and I will question Clifford, Little Red Riding Hood, and Peter Rabbit. You two guys question Curious George, the Big Bad Wolf, and the little pig."

She quickly wrote out a list of questions they should ask:

1. Did you leave the library during the dedication party?
2. Did you go back into your classroom?
3. If so, why did you go in?
4. Did you see anyone else go in or out of the classroom?
5. If so, who?

Fill in the names of the suspects on their question sheets below and on the following page. Then, look back at the testimony by Mrs. Mills on p. 23 to help you analyze the students' answers to the questions and find the most likely suspect or suspects.

Clifford

Name_____

Answers:
1. Yes
2. Yes
3. I went with my friend to get part of her costume.
4. Yes
5. Laura was with me.

Curious George

Name_____

Answers:
1. Yes
2. No
3. Did not answer.
4. Yes
5. I saw Miguel coming out of the classroom.

Little Red Riding Hood

Name_____

Answers:
1. Yes
2. Yes
3. To get my basket.
4. No, just us.
5. Andrew was with me.

The Big Bad Wolf

Name_____

Answers:
1. Yes
2. Yes
3. I went with Jacob.
4. Yes
5. I saw Jacob go in, but I didn't wait for him to go out.

Peter Rabbit

Name_____

Answers:
1. Yes
2. Yes
3. To get Mrs. Brady's camera off her desk.
4. Not exactly going in.
5. Douglas was going toward the room.

Little Pig

Name_____

Answers:
1. Yes
2. Yes
3. Zach couldn't find his wand. I told him I would see if he left in the room.
4. Yes
5. Juan.

When they had finished questioning their suspects, the detectives got together and analyzed the answers. They decided who was the most likely person to have taken Dominic's gold medal.

Who do you think took the medal? _____

Why do you think that person is the most likely suspect? _____

_____

_____

When they confronted their suspect, he admitted he had been jealous of Dominic's prize. "I never intended to wear it myself, I just didn't want to see Dominic showing off. I hid the medal in the bottom of the wastebasket. I'm really sorry!" he apologized.

The detectives found the hidden medal and returned it to Dominic. He was happy to get it back, and was impressed with the detectives' quick work. He thanked Sara over and over for getting the Detective Club on the case.

The Case of the Missing Medal
Teacher's Guide

Sara and the Summer Reading Club (p. 21)

Introduce Shirley Sharp's younger sister, Sara, and discuss why she's so glad to be in Mrs. Brady's class. Direct students to solve the puzzle on p. 21 that Mrs. Brady made up for her class. Point out that it is similar to the logic puzzles they did on Shirley's tests. Mention that there are two boys in the puzzle, Jacob and Dominic, and three girls, Sarah, Patricia, and Tenille. Remind the students that "nos" are very important, and ask them how many "nos" they can fill in from the first clue (Tenille cannot be first, and none of the girls can be third.). *Note:* It may help students to interpret clues with "more" and "fewer," like the ones in this puzzle, by writing the names in a hierarchy. For example: For clue one, write "Tenille" and "boy in 3rd" on one line, then write "Dominic" above them. This will help students see that Tenille could not have been first, because Dominic is above her, and Dominic could not have been fourth or fifth, because two people were lower than him.

Answers: Jacob placed third; Dominic placed first; Tenille placed second; Sara placed fifth; and Patricia placed fourth.

The Costume Party (pp. 22–23)

Discuss the circumstances of the medal disappearing during the party. On pp. 22–23, have the students circle or underline the six characters Mrs. Mills saw going into the classroom during that time: Little Red Riding Hood, Clifford, Peter Rabbit, Curious George, the Big Bad Wolf, and a little pig.

Costume Party Puzzle 1 (p. 24)

Before students begin the puzzle on p. 24, ask them if they are familiar with all of the storybook characters in this puzzle, and if they know which names are girls' names and which are boys' names. If any have difficulty solving the puzzle, go over the first clue with them and make sure they have recorded all the possible information from this clue ("nos" for all the girls for Arthur and Clifford, "nos" for the boys for all the other costumes).

Answers: Laura is Little Red Riding Hood; Patricia is D. W.; Andrew is Clifford; Brendan is Arthur; Jane is Francine; and Tenille is Goldilocks.

Costume Party Puzzle 2 (p. 25)

As in the previous puzzle, make sure the students are familiar with the storybook characters and know which students are girls and boys.

Answers: Douglas is Curious George; Hannah is Amelia Bedelia; Mary is Cinderella; Daniel is Nate the Great; Elizabeth is Miss Frizzle; and Miguel is Peter Rabbit.

Costume Party Puzzle 3 (p. 26)

As in the previous puzzles, make sure the students are familiar with the storybook characters and know which students are girls and boys.

Answers: Tayshawn is Happy; Dominic is Dopey; Hailey is Grumpy; Katherine is Sneezy; Jacob is the Little Pig; and Sara is Snow White.

Costume Party Puzzle 4 (p. 27)

As in the previous puzzles, make sure the students are familiar with the storybook characters and know which students are girls and boys.

Answers: Zachary is Harry Potter; Stephanie is The Grinch; Juan is the Big Bad Wolf; Choya is the Cat in the Hat; Janelle is the Wicked Witch; and Brett is a Berenstain Bear.

Cracking the Case (pp. 28–29)

After the students fill in the names of the suspects on their questions sheets on pp. 28–29, have them compare the answers each suspect gave to Mrs. Mills to conclude who is the most likely suspect.

Answers: Clifford is Andrew, Little Red Riding Hood is Laura, Curious George is Douglas, the Big Bad Wolf is Juan, Peter Rabbit is Miguel, and the little pig is Jacob; they are the six suspects. The most likely suspect is Douglas, because he lied when he said he did not go back into the classroom. Miguel saw him going toward the classroom, and Mrs. Mills saw him go into the classroom.

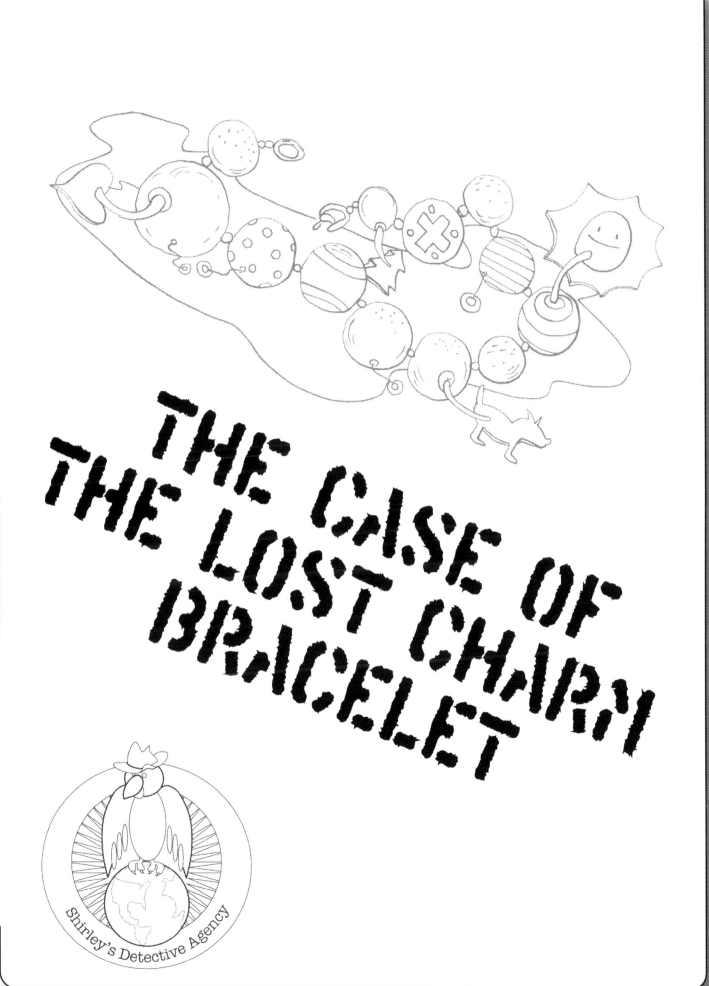

THE CASE OF THE LOST CHARM BRACELET

Shirley's Detective Agency

The Case of the Lost Charm Bracelet
Finding the Bracelet

Bill and Betty Bright's mother worked Saturday mornings at the Fairfield Park District where there were many different activities offered for kids. Bill and Betty went with her, and enjoyed the activities they had signed up for. Shirley Sharp went too. She and Betty played soccer, did crafts, and then took swimming lessons. Shirley and Betty were becoming good swimmers. Their teacher, Miss Finn, had moved them up from the Minnows group to the Dolphins.

One day after swimming lessons, while they were waiting for Mrs. Bright to finish work, the girls were helping Miss Finn in the locker room. As they were helping put things away, Shirley

noticed something shiny under one of the locker room benches. It was a silver charm bracelet.

"Betty!" she called. "Come see what I found."

"Wow!" said Betty. "That's cool! It looks like an expensive bracelet. I wonder who lost it."

"We're detectives," Shirley replied. "Let's see if we can solve the mystery and find the owner. The charms on the bracelet will be good clues."

The girls looked closely at the silver charms: a soccer ball, a baseball bat, a letter J, a music note, a dog, Mickey Mouse, and a heart with a red ruby.

"Where do we start?" asked Betty.

"Let's start with the easiest, the letter J," Shirley answered. "The owner's name probably starts with the letter J."

"Right!" said Betty. "Let's check the lists of swimming classes that took place this morning."

The girls hurried over to the bulletin board where the class lists were posted, and checked the three classes. The three groups that had met that morning were the Minnows, the Dolphins, and the Sharks.

Shirley, who always carried her detective notebook with her, got it out of her backpack. At the top of a page she wrote, "The Case of the Lost Charm Bracelet." The girls checked over the class lists. Betty read off all of the girls who had first or last names that started with a J. Shirley wrote them all down.

Check the lists below and write down the names with a "J" initial on the Possible Owners Sheet on the next page. Remember, an initial can represent someone's first or last name.

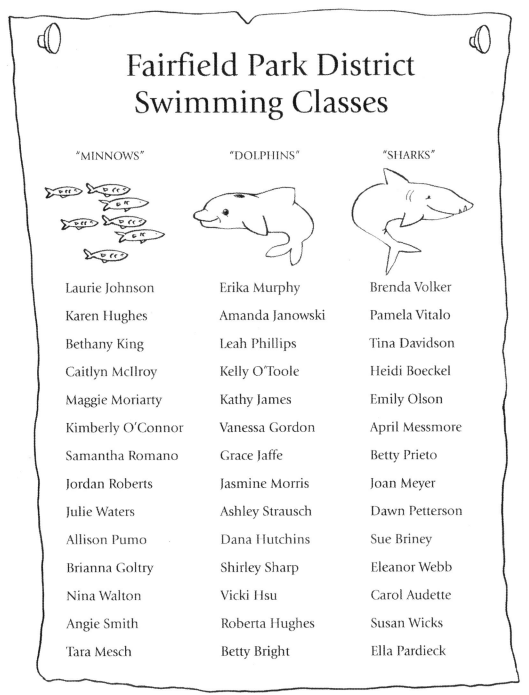

Fairfield Park District Swimming Classes

"MINNOWS"	"DOLPHINS"	"SHARKS"
Laurie Johnson	Erika Murphy	Brenda Volker
Karen Hughes	Amanda Janowski	Pamela Vitalo
Bethany King	Leah Phillips	Tina Davidson
Caitlyn McIlroy	Kelly O'Toole	Heidi Boeckel
Maggie Moriarty	Kathy James	Emily Olson
Kimberly O'Connor	Vanessa Gordon	April Messmore
Samantha Romano	Grace Jaffe	Betty Prieto
Jordan Roberts	Jasmine Morris	Joan Meyer
Julie Waters	Ashley Strausch	Dawn Petterson
Allison Pumo	Dana Hutchins	Sue Briney
Brianna Goltry	Shirley Sharp	Eleanor Webb
Nina Walton	Vicki Hsu	Carol Audette
Angie Smith	Roberta Hughes	Susan Wicks
Tara Mesch	Betty Bright	Ella Pardieck

The Case of the Lost Charm Bracelet
Possible Owners

Laurie Johnson ♡

The Case of the Lost Charm Bracelet
Charm Clue Chart

As Shirley looked over the list she had made, she realized they would need to organize the information they collected. She and Betty made this chart to do so. Use the chart to record the names of the eight girls who have a first or last name that starts with "J." You can put a check mark in the "Letter J" column for each of them. As you and the detectives track down more information, record the information on the chart.

Name	Soccer Ball	Baseball Bat	Letter J	Music Note	Dog	Mickey Mouse	Ruby Heart

The Case of the Lost Charm Bracelet
July Birthdays

When they had completed their list, Betty asked, "What's next?"

"I've been thinking about the charm with the ruby," Shirley said thoughtfully. "I know that the ruby is the birthstone for July."

"So, we need to find out who has a birthday in July," said Betty.

The Fairfield Park District has a big birthday party every month to celebrate all of the birthdays in that month. Every three months, they put up birthday puzzles, one for the boys and one for the girls. Anyone who takes a copy of the puzzle and solves it correctly gets a prize.

"Let's check the girls' birthday puzzle," said Shirley. "We're in luck, because the one that's up now is for July, August, and September."

When you find the girls who have July birthdays, record the information on the Charm Clue Chart on p. 35.

Girls' Birthday Puzzle	July 4	July 12	July 16	July 21	July 28	July 30	Aug. 3	Aug. 4	Aug. 12	Sept. 12	Sept. 28
Laurie Johnson											
Caitlyn McIlroy											
Kathy James											
Julie Waters											
Jordan Roberts											
Grace Jaffe											
Amanda Janowski											
Joan Meyer											
Brenda Volker											
Jasmine Morris											
Angie Smith											

Clues

1. Laurie and Grace are the only two girls who have their birthdays after Labor Day.

2. Jasmine, Kathy, and Laurie each have a birthday on the 12th, but in different months.

3. Joan's birthday is on a holiday.

4. Julie's birthday is one week (7 days) after Jordan's.

5. Brenda's birthday is the day after Caitlyn's.

6. Amanda's birthday is after Jasmine's, but before Angie's.

The Case of the Lost Charm Bracelet
Studying the Class Enrollment Cards

"OK, so we have five girls with the initial 'J' who have July birthdays. What's next?" Betty asked.

"We need to get some information about the interests of those five girls so we can decide who might have the other charms on her bracelet," Shirley replied.

"Maybe if we could find out what other classes these girls have signed up for, we could learn something about their interests and what charms they might have," Betty suggested.

So, they went to the office where Mrs. Bright was working and asked for her help. She showed them the enrollment cards for the five girls.

Study the cards and decide what charms each girl might have, based on the classes she has signed up to take. Record the information on the Charm Clue Chart on p. 35.

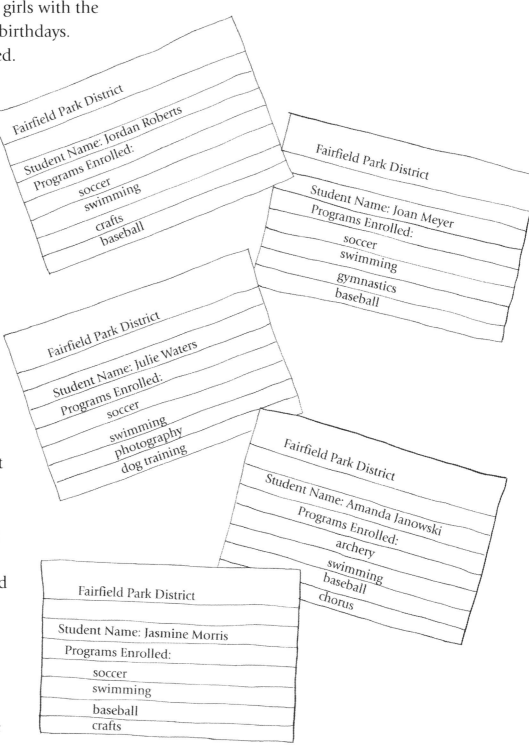

Fairfield Park District

Student Name: Jordan Roberts
Programs Enrolled:

soccer
swimming

crafts
baseball

Fairfield Park District

Student Name: Joan Meyer
Programs Enrolled:

soccer
swimming
gymnastics
baseball

Fairfield Park District

Student Name: Julie Waters
Programs Enrolled:

soccer
swimming
photography
dog training

Fairfield Park District

Student Name: Amanda Janowski
Programs Enrolled:
archery
swimming
baseball
chorus

Fairfield Park District

Student Name: Jasmine Morris
Programs Enrolled:
soccer
swimming
baseball
crafts

The Case of the Lost Charm Bracelet
Getting More Information

While Betty and Shirley were in the office, three of the counselors stopped by on their way to lunch. Shirley saw another opportunity for getting some information.

She showed the bracelet to the counselors. None of them knew who it belonged to. Shirley explained that she and Betty were trying to solve the mystery.

"We think the bracelet belongs to either Jordan, Julie, Amanda Janowski, Joan, or Jasmine," she told them. "Those five all have the initial 'J' and also have a birthday in July."

Mrs. Wang looked at the bracelet and remembered that Julie and Jordan's baseball team played against Amanda and Joan's team in the championship game last year. She also knew that Jordan and Jasmine take piano lessons.

Mrs. Kelly knew that Julie, Jasmine, Amanda, and Joan play on the same soccer team as her daughter Shannon.

Miss Sanchez remembered that when Joan's dog had puppies, she gave one to Julie and one to Jasmine. Miss Sanchez also belongs to the same church that Joan and Julie go to and said that both girls sing in the Junior Choir.

Shirley thanked the counselors for the valuable information.

"Let's get this info down on our Charm Clue Chart," said Betty excitedly. "Maybe the mystery is solved."

"I don't think so," said Shirley. "We still have the Mickey Mouse charm to investigate."

Record the information Shirley and Betty discovered on your Charm Clue Chart on p. 35.

The Case of the Lost Charm Bracelet
Vacation Postcards

As they left the office, Shirley's eyes lit up when she saw the postcards on the vacation bulletin board across the hall.

"Aha! We may find the final piece of the puzzle right here on this bulletin board," she told Betty. "I bet the Mickey Mouse charm is a souvenir from Disneyland or Disney World."

"Wow! Good thinking! Disneyland is in California and Disney World is in Florida. We can see if any of the five girls sent a postcard from one of those states."

Use the following information about the postcards to find out which state each girl visited.

1. Amanda's postcard was of a very tall building called The Sears Tower.

   She visited the state of _____.

2. Jordan's postcard was of the Golden Gate Bridge.

   She visited the state of _____.

3. Julie's postcard was of the Lincoln Memorial and Jasmine's was of Lincoln's tomb.

   Julie visited _____.

   Jasmine visited the state of _____.

4. Joan's postcard showed rockets at Cape Canaveral.

   She visited the state of _____.

From what you learned from the postcards, which two girls are most likely to have bought a Mickey Mouse charm on their vacation?

_____ and _____

Record this information on your Charm Clue Chart on p. 35.

The Case of the Lost Charm Bracelet
Solving the Mystery

When Betty and Shirley looked over all the information on their Charm Clue Chart, they agreed on whom the bracelet probably belonged to.

Be sure you have recorded on the Charm Clue Chart all the information you have learned.

When you look at all of the information, to whom do you think the bracelet belongs?

_____

How did you reach your conclusion? _____

_____

_____

_____

_____

When the girls showed Mrs. Bright their clue chart and explained how they reached their conclusion, she was impressed with their good detective work. She called the girl's house right away.

They were right. The girl and her mother were so excited to hear her bracelet had been found that they offered a reward to Betty and Shirley.

"No, thanks," said Shirley. "It's all in a day's work for members of the Detective Club."

As the girls high-fived each other, Mrs. Bright congratulated them on a job well done.

The Case of the Lost Charm Bracelet
Teacher's Guide

Finding the Bracelet (pp. 32–33)

Introduce the park district's Saturday classes scenario on p. 32. Have students share their ideas about how the charms might help Betty and Shirley find the owner of the lost bracelet.

Direct students to analyze the class lists on p. 33 and have them record all the names with a "J" initial on the notebook sheet provided. The eight names are Laurie Johnson, Kathy James, Jordan Roberts, Grace Jaffe, Julie Waters, Jasmine Morris, Amanda Janowski, and Joan Meyer.

Clue Charm Chart (p. 35)

Direct students to begin the chart on p. 35 by writing in the first names of the eight girls they recorded on the previous page and putting a check mark in the "Letter J" column for each one. The students will fill this out further as they go along.

July Birthdays (p. 36)

Discuss how the ruby charm led Shirley to deduce that the owner's birthday is in July. Introduce the park district's puzzle for July, August, and September birthdays on p. 36. Have students solve the puzzle and put check marks in the "Ruby Heart" column of their Charm Clue Chart (p. 35) for each girl who has a July birthday. Answers: Laurie Johnson was born on September 12; Caitlyn McIlroy was born on August 3; Kathy James was born on August 12; Julie Waters was born on July 28; Jordan Roberts was born on July 21; Grace Jaffe was born on September 28; Amanda Janowski was born on July 16; Joan Meyer was born on July 4; Brenda Volker was born on August 4; Jasmine Morris was born on July 12; and Angie Smith was born on July 30.

Studying the Class Enrollment Cards (p. 37)

Direct students to analyze the enrollment cards of the five girls with a July birthday and a "J" initial on p. 37, looking for information about their interests. From the information given, they can infer the following charms for the five girls: Jordan—soccer ball and baseball bat; Julie—soccer ball and dog; Amanda—baseball bat and music note; Jasmine—soccer ball and baseball bat; and Joan—soccer ball and baseball bat.

Direct students to mark check marks for the above findings in their charts.

Getting More Information (p. 38)

Direct students to analyze the information given by the three counselors on p. 38. This information should lead them to add the following check marks to their charts: Amanda—soccer ball; Jordan—music note; Jasmine—dog and music note; Julie—baseball bat and music note; and Joan—baseball bat, dog, and music note.

Vacation Postcards (p. 39)

Introduce the vacation bulletin board on p. 39. Discuss ways students can figure out from what state each of the five girls sent her postcard (i.e., Web search, library, etc).

Answers: Amanda visited Illinois; Jordan visited California; Julie visited Washington, DC; Jasmine visited Illinois; and Joan visited Florida.

The girls most like to have the Mickey Mouse charm are Jordan and Joan.

(Have students add those checks to their charts.)

Solving the Mystery (p. 40)

Direct students to analyze the information they have recorded on their charts so far and reach a conclusion as to who owns the bracelet.

Answer: Joan Meyer, because she is the only one who has a check mark for every charm.

Final Charm Clue Chart:

	S. Ball	Bat	"J"	Note	Dog	M.M.	Ruby
Laurie Johnson			✔				
Jordan Roberts	✔	✔	✔	✔		✔	✔
Julie Waters	✔	✔	✔	✔	✔		✔
Amanda Janowski	✔	✔	✔	✔			✔
Kathy Jones			✔				
Grace Jaffe			✔				
Jasmine Morris	✔	✔	✔	✔	✔		✔
Joan Meyer	✔	✔	✔	✔	✔	✔	✔

THE CASE OF THE MISSING MASCOT

Shirley's Detective Agency

The Case of the Missing Mascot
Tommy Tiger Disappears

Cory Quest was waiting for his sister, Carrie, to finish her afterschool practice with the Fairfield North cheerleaders. They were getting ready for Saturday's big football game. The Fairfield North Tigers were playing their crosstown rivals, the Fairfield South Lions.

Austin, who dressed as the Tiger mascot for all of the games, went to the locker room to put on the Tommy Tiger costume. Imagine his surprise when he discovered it was gone! In its place was a large sign that read:

If you are looking for Tommy Tiger, check out the goal post on the south end of the football field.
—Leo the Lion

Austin grabbed the sign and ran into the gym to show it to the cheerleaders. "Someone is playing a trick on us." Carrie said, "Look! It's signed 'Leo the Lion.' I'll bet the Fairfield South cheerleaders took our mascot."

"What are we waiting for?" asked Austin. "Let's go get our tiger."

All of the cheerleaders followed Austin as he ran out to the football field, with Cory right behind them.

When they got to the south goal post, they were disappointed. Tommy Tiger was nowhere in sight, but taped to the goal post was an envelope marked "Clue 1." Inside the envelope they found a message that made no sense. "Oh, no! It's written in code," groaned Austin.

Cory, a new member of the Detective Club, spoke up, "This is getting interesting."

The cheerleaders and Austin did not agree. They were all muttering to each other:

"Interesting? Not to me! I hate codes!"

"We don't have time for puzzles, we have work to do on our new cheers!"

"We have to find our mascot before the big game on Saturday!"

Cory whispered in his sister's ear, "This is a good case for the Detective Club to tackle while you all go ahead with your cheerleading practice."

"Good idea, Cory," she agreed.

When she told the others Cory's idea, they all gladly agreed to turn the case over to the Detective Club. Cory called the other members of the Detective Club to work on the case with him. They hopped on their bikes and came right over.

Cory showed them the note and the detectives began to analyze the code. Shirley noticed that there were no numbers above 26 in the code. "I'll bet the numbers have something to do with the alphabet," she said.

"Maybe A = 1, B = 2, and so on," Bill suggested.

"That can't be right," said Betty. "There are no ones in the clue, and I'm sure there would be at least one 'A' in it."

"Well, I still think the numbers relate to the alphabet in some way," Shirley insisted. "Let's think of other possibilities."

Can you break the code?

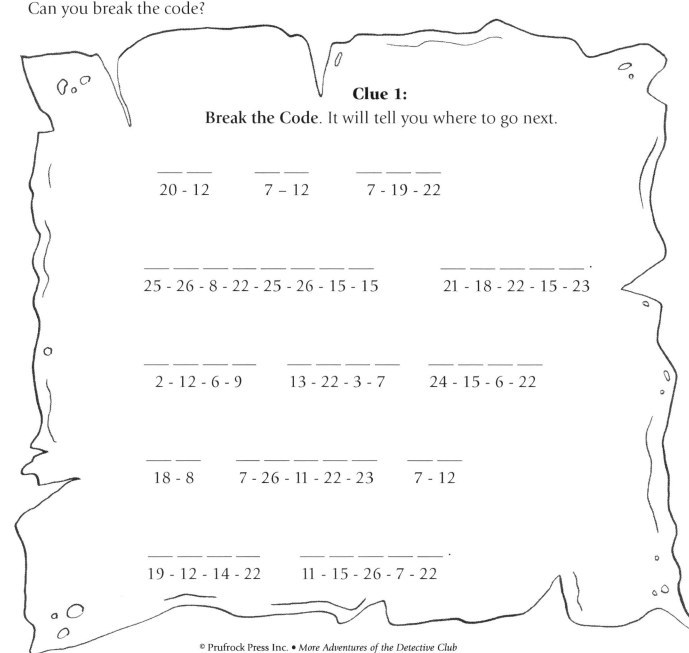

Clue 1:

Break the Code. It will tell you where to go next.

___ ___   ___ ___   ___ ___ ___
20 - 12   7 – 12   7 - 19 - 22

___ ___ ___ ___ ___ ___ ___ ___   ___ ___ ___ ___ ___.
25 - 26 - 8 - 22 - 25 - 26 - 15 - 15   21 - 18 - 22 - 15 - 23

___ ___ ___ ___   ___ ___ ___ ___   ___ ___ ___ ___
2 - 12 - 6 - 9   13 - 22 - 3 - 7   24 - 15 - 6 - 22

___ ___   ___ ___ ___ ___ ___   ___ ___
18 - 8   7 - 26 - 11 - 22 - 23   7 - 12

___ ___ ___ ___   ___ ___ ___ ___ ___.
19 - 12 - 14 - 22   11 - 15 - 26 - 7 - 22

The Case of the Missing Mascot
Inside the Second Clue

When the detectives decoded the message, they went right to the spot and found the envelope marked "Clue 2." This is what they found inside the envelope:

You will find Clue 3 under a seat at the football stadium. Solve the puzzles below to find the location of the seat.

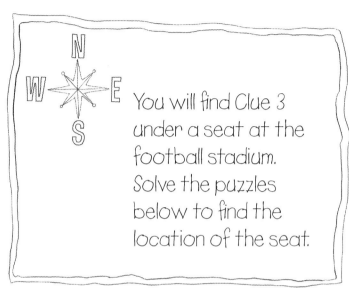

You will find Clue 3 under a seat at the football stadium. Solve the puzzles below to find the location of the seat.

Side of the field: Stand on the 50-yard line facing south. Take three steps forward. Turn to your left and take three steps. Now, turn to your right and take two steps. Turn right again and take three steps. Turn left, take two steps, and then turn left again. What direction are you facing? East or West (Circle one).

Sections (A to Z): Read the clues below to figure out what section to look in.

1. The letter is in *Washington*, but not in *Ohio*. (Write the possible letters below, then eliminate from this pool using the other clues.)

2. The letter is in *West Virginia*, but not in *Wyoming*.
3. The letter is in *Texas*, but not in *Indiana*.
4. The letter is in *Massachusetts*, but not in *Vermont*.

The section is letter _____.

Name:_____ Date:_____

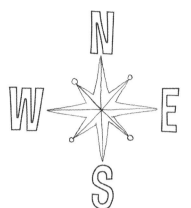

Row Number: The row is a two-digit number. The first digit is an even number and the second digit is an odd number. The sum of the digits is seven. The second digit is greater than that first digit. The row is number _____.

Seat Number: Start with 10, divide by 2: _____

Take that number and add 3: _____

Double that number: _____

Add 4 to that number: _____

Divide by 2: _____

The seat number is _____.

Clue 3 is taped under Seat _____, in Row _____,

of Section _____, on the _____ side of the field.

Name:_____ Date:_____

The Case of the Missing Mascot
Visiting the Cheerleaders' Homes

Betty Bright, who was always eager to beat her brother Bill, got to the right seat first and found the clue taped underneath. As the other detectives gathered around, she read, "Clue 4 is at the home of one of the Fairfield South cheerleaders. Go to Marty's house to pick it up."

"How are we supposed to know where that is?" Bill interrupted.

"Let me finish, Bill. Here's the puzzle we need to solve to answer that question."

Cheerleaders' Homes	2312 Oak	1809 Main	2419 Pine	607 Third	802 First	2428 Birch
Amber						
Marty						
Sophia						
Leslie						
Maui						
Christopher						

Clues

1. The two boys, Marty and Christopher, live on the numbered streets.
2. Maui's street has the same number of letters as her name.
3. Sophia's street is not named after a tree, but Leslie's is.
4. Amber's house number does not have a 1 in it, and Marty's does not have a 2.

Marty's address is _____.

The Case of the Missing Mascot
The Final Clue

When the Detective Club figured out where Marty lived, they were feeling good! They felt they were closing in on the case. They asked Cory's sister, Carrie, to drive them to the house. She was happy to help get Tommy Tiger back.

When they arrived at Marty's house, his mother answered the door and gave them an envelope marked "Clue 4." Inside the envelope was this note:

Clue 4: Congratulations! You have almost reached the end of the trail. Tommy Tiger is waiting for you at the home of one of the Fairfield South football players. Solve the next three puzzles to rescue Tommy Tiger. Good luck!

"Wow! Three more puzzles to go," Carrie said. "They look pretty hard. Do you think you can solve them?"

"Are you kidding? We're great at logic puzzles," Cory replied. "Of course we can do it."

"OK, let's do it!" said Bill, and they got right to work on the three puzzles in Clue 4.

The Case of the Missing Mascot
Team Addresses, Puzzle 1

Team Address	3080 Ninth	4710 Sixth	5025 Second	509 Pine	671 Oak	707 Ash
Mark						
Ben						
Dillon						
Mason						
Joel						
D. J.						

Use the clues below to find out where these Fairfield South players live.

Clues
1. Mason and Joel have addresses that end with zero, but only Mason's house number has more than one zero in it.
2. Dillon's house number is higher than Ben's, but lower than Mark's, and all three of them have house numbers that add up to 14.

The Case of the Missing Mascot
Team Addresses, Puzzle 2

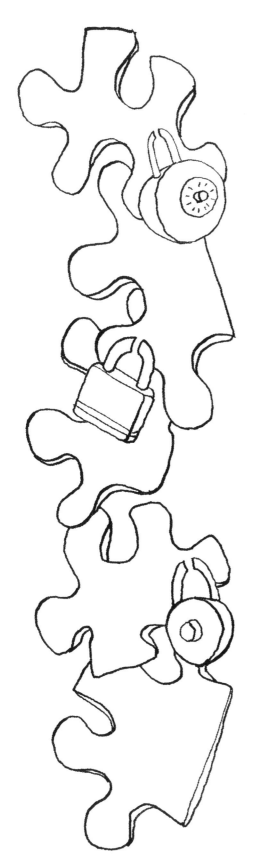

Use the clues below to find out where these Fairfield South players live.

Team Addresses	2442 Third	1019 First	3773 Fifth	342 Cedar	871 Maple
Veejay					
Keeshon					
Scott					
Mike					
Jose					

Clues
1. Veejay and Keeshon have house numbers that are palindromes: They read the same forward and backward.
2. Jose's house number is higher than Mike's, but lower than Scott's.
3. Keeshon, Scott, and Jose have addresses that are odd numbers.

The Case of the Missing Mascot
Which Player Has Tommy Tiger?

After solving the team address puzzles, the kids found they weren't done yet. They still had to figure out which player had Tommy Tiger. Another sheet was attached to the puzzles with the following information:

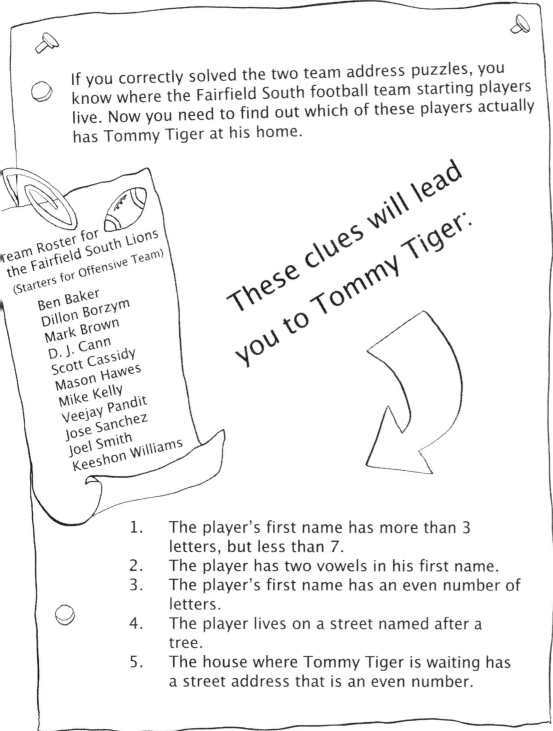

If you correctly solved the two team address puzzles, you know where the Fairfield South football team starting players live. Now you need to find out which of these players actually has Tommy Tiger at his home.

Team Roster for the Fairfield South Lions
(Starters for Offensive Team)

Ben Baker
Dillon Borzym
Mark Brown
D. J. Cann
Scott Cassidy
Mason Hawes
Mike Kelly
Veejay Pandit
Jose Sanchez
Joel Smith
Keeshon Williams

These clues will lead you to Tommy Tiger:

1. The player's first name has more than 3 letters, but less than 7.
2. The player has two vowels in his first name.
3. The player's first name has an even number of letters.
4. The player lives on a street named after a tree.
5. The house where Tommy Tiger is waiting has a street address that is an even number.

When they learned that Tommy was at _____'s house, they had Carrie drive them right there. When they got there, they found Tommy Tiger propped up on a chair on the porch! They quickly rescued him and drove back to the Fairfield North field.

When the cheerleaders saw the detectives with the Tiger suit, they cheered:

THREE CHEERS FOR THE DETECTIVE CLUB! HIP, HIP, HOORAY!

The Case of the Missing Mascot
Teacher's Guide

Tommy Tiger Disappears (pp. 43–44)

Introduce the scenario of the cheerleaders discovering their team mascot's costume is missing on p. 43. Discuss the sign that was left in its place, which led them to the coded message on p. 44.

Ask the students if they have ever been on a treasure hunt where one clue led to another until they reached the "treasure." Point out that the message marked "Clue 1" is not a cryptogram, but a **coded** message that will tell them where to go to find Clue 2.

The code is in alphabetical position, but in reverse order (A = 26, Z = 1). Answer: Go to the baseball field. Your next clue is taped to home plate.

Inside the Second Clue (pp. 45–46)

Direct students to solve the puzzles on pp. 45–46 to find the seat under which the clue is hidden. In finding the side of the field, encourage students to use the compass provided or another compass to plot their steps. The students should find the direction to be East. For the section letter, students will first pull out the letters W, A, S, N, G, and T (in Washington, but not in Ohio). Then, from that group they eliminate the letters W, N, and G (in West Virginia, but not in Wyoming). Next, they eliminate A (in Texas, but not in Indiana). Finally, they eliminate T (in Massachusetts, but not in Vermont). Instruct the students to use logic to solve the Row Number riddle, and then help them use calculations to solve the Seat Number equation (some may need calculators for the division, depending on the age range you're using this book with). Students now have the coordinates for the next clue. Answers: East side of the field, Section S, Row 25, Seat 10.

Visiting the Cheerleaders' Homes (p. 47)

Direct the students to solve the matrix logic puzzle on p. 47 to find each cheerleader's address. Answers: Amber lives at 2428 Birch; Marty lives at 607 Third; Sophia lives at 1809 Main; Leslie lives at 2312 Oak; Maui lives at 2419 Pine; Christopher lives at 802 First.

The Final Clue (p. 48)

Discuss Clue 4 on p. 48. Direct students to solve the matrix logic puzzles on pp. 49–51 to find each football player's address. These two logic puzzles have clues pertaining to the house numbers, rather than the streets where the players live. Students will use their knowledge of odd and even numbers, finding sums, and comparing numerical values to solve these puzzles.

Team Addresses, Puzzle 1 (p. 49)

Answers: Mark lives at 707 Ash; Ben lives at 509 Pine; Dillon lives at 671 Oak; Mason lives at 3080 Ninth; Joel lives at 4710 Sixth; and D. J. lives at 5025 Second.

Team Addresses, Puzzle 2 (p. 50)

Answers: Veejay lives at 2442 Third; Keeshon lives at 3773 Fifth; Scott lives at 1019 First; Mike lives at 342 Cedar; and Jose lives at 871 Maple.

Which Player Has Tommy Tiger? (p. 51)

Direct students to use the clues on p. 51, the answers to the two address puzzles, and the team roster to find out which of the football players has the tiger costume at his house.

Answer: The costume is at Mike Kelly's house.

THE CASE OF THE TREASURE HUNT

The Case of the Treasure Hunt
The End-of-the-Year Party

Bill and Cory's teacher was planning a special end-of-the-year party for their class. He asked the students to be thinking about possible ideas for activities.

As Bill and Cory walked home, they talked about the upcoming party. Cory stopped. "Do you remember how much fun we had following the clues to find the missing mascot?"

"That was cool," Bill answered. "Maybe we could do something like a treasure hunt for our class party."

"It would be a lot of work, but we could always get Betty and Shirley to help us," added Cory.

The next morning, they shared their idea with their teacher, Mr. Sparrow. He thought it would be an excellent activity, because the kids would be thinking critically, while having fun.

The next day was Saturday, so the boys called a morning meeting of the Detective Club. They explained their treasure hunt idea to Shirley and Betty and asked for their help.

"Sounds like a lot of work," said Betty. "But, I think it will be fun."

"I think so too." Shirley agreed. "Let's get started!"

"Where do we start?" the boys asked her.

"Well, before we write any clues," answered Shirley, "we have to think about where in the school we could hide clues."

They brainstormed several places in and around the school where they might hide clues. Then they talked about what type of clues they could give.

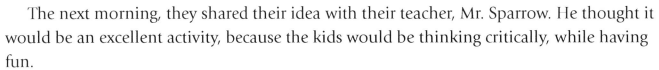

"Let's make up some puzzles like those Shirley made up for us to solve when we became members of the Detective Club," Bill suggested.

So, they set to work planning their treasure hunt and creating clues.

See if you can follow the clues they wrote and find the treasure.

The Case of the Treasure Hunt
Solving the First Clue

On the day of the party, the class was divided into teams. Each team was given an envelope with its team number on it. The envelopes were marked "Clue 1." This is what they found inside the envelope:

Your team will find Clue 2 in an envelope hidden in a book in the library. When you find the book, take the envelope with your team number on it. Then, follow the instructions given in Clue 2 to find the third clue.

The book where you will find Clue 2 is about a person who:
- was a president of the United States,
- has a last name that begins with G,
- was president some time after Abraham Lincoln was president,
- was president some time before Grover Cleveland was president, and
- was born in 1822.

The answer is in a book about President _____.

Name:_____ Date:_____

The Case of the Treasure Hunt
Cracking Clue 2's Cryptic Message

The teams used their sharp deductive skills, the classroom encyclopedias, and the online encyclopedias on their class computer to discover that they had to find a book about President Grant in the library. Next, they went to the library and searched through the card catalog until they found all of the books on President Grant. Teams hunted carefully through the books until they found their next clue. Can you figure out where Clue 3 will be hidden based on the puzzle in Clue 2 below?

This clue is a **Cryptogram Puzzle.**

Each letter in the puzzle represents some other letter in the alphabet. For instance, in the puzzle below N = T and L = H. Solve the Cryptogram Puzzle to answer the question: Where is the next clue?

U N ' R   L U J J O V   U V   N L O

__ __ ' __   __ __ __ __ __ __   __ __   __ __ __

V A C R O ' R   I D D U T O ,   E V

__ __ __ __ __ ' __   __ __ __ __ __ __ , __ __

L O C   J O R Q .

__ __ __   __ __ __ __ .

Name:_____ Date:_____

The Case of the Treasure Hunt
Seeking Out Other Students

The students thought carefully about the cryptic code in Clue 2. After a few minutes, one team jumped up and rushed off to the nurse's office. They had cracked the code! Clue 3 was sitting on the nurse's desk. Here's what it said:

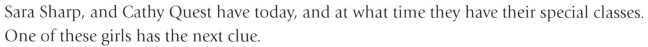

To find your next clue, you will need to solve the logic puzzle below. The puzzle will tell you what two special classes Shirley Sharp, Betty Bright, Sara Sharp, and Cathy Quest have today, and at what time they have their special classes. One of these girls has the next clue.

All four of them have physical education class today. Two have art today and two have music. The person who has the next clue has art class at 10:45 a.m.

Special Class	Physical Education at 9:00 a.m.	Physical Education at 9:30 a.m.	Physical Education at 10:00 a.m.	Physical Education at 2:00 p.m.	Art at 10:45 a.m.	Art at 1:00 p.m.	Music at 9:00 a.m.	Music at 9:45 a.m.
Shirley Sharp								
Betty Bright								
Sara Sharp								
Cathy Quest								

Clues
1. Shirley has physical education at the same time Betty has music.
2. Cathy has physical education before Shirley has art, and Betty has physical education before Cathy has music.
3. Sara has physical education and art in the afternoon.

The person who has art class at 10:45 a.m. is _____.

The Case of the Treasure Hunt
Unscrambling Clue 4

Shirley received lots of requests for Clue 4 once the students solved the logic puzzle. But, the students still had more challenging puzzles to go. Clue 4 contained a tough anagram puzzle. Can you solve it?

In this word puzzle, all of the correct letters are in each word, but they have been scrambled. Unscramble the letters to find the location of Clue 4.

HET   LRAOGYNUDP   SI   EWEHR

_____ _____ ____ _____

UCEL   REMNBU   VEIF   SI   DEHNID.

_____ _____ _____ ____ _____.

TI   SI   PDEAT   EDNRU   ETH

____ ____ _____ _____ ____

TASE   FO   EHT   LIMDED

_____ ____ ____ _____

SNGWI.

_____.

© Prufrock Press Inc. • *More Adventures of the Detective Club*

The Case of the Treasure Hunt
Visiting Classrooms

The clue on the playground had these directions: A student named Michael has the next clue in his desk. You can find out what class he is in by solving this logic puzzle:

	Pedro	Dong Mei	Kyle	Julia	Luke	Michael	Justin	Ling	Gabriel	
										Ms. Springer, Grade 3
										Ms. Gonzales, Grade 3
										Ms. Hawes, Grade 3
										Ms. Dorn, Grade 4
										Ms. Steinbach, Grade 4
										Mr. Dresdow, Grade 4
										Ms. Strum, Grade 5
										Mr. Delaney, Grade 5
										Mr. Sing, Grade 5

Clues:
1. Gabriel and Justin's teachers' last names begin with "S," but Kyle and Michael's do not.
2. Julia is in a higher grade than Gabriel, but lower than Pedro.
3. Ling's sister, Dong Mei, is two grades ahead of her.
4. Dong Mei, who is not in Mr. Sing's class, is in a higher grade than Justin.
5. Luke's teacher's last name begins with "D," but Michael's does not.
6. Luke walks to school with the boy in Mr. Dresdow's class, the girl in Ms. Dorn's class, and the boy in Ms. Hawes' class.

Michael is in _____class.

The Case of the Treasure Hunt
Finally, the Treasure!

Michael had a lot of visitors to his class. The students were so excited to open the clue he had and find that it was the last clue. They were so close to finding the treasure! Can you solve the clue and figure out where the treasure is hidden?

This is your last clue. It will lead you to the treasure. Solve the number puzzle below to find the room number where the treasure awaits you.

1. Write the correct number in the blanks:
    a. A two-digit number. Both digits are even. The second digit is twice as big as the first digit. The number is less than 36. The number is _____
    b. A three-digit odd number. The first two digits are the same even number. The sum of the three digits is 17. The third digit is one less than the second digit. The number is _____
    c. A three-digit odd number. The first digit is one more than the second digit. The second digit is one more than the third digit. The sum of the digits is 18. The number is

    _____

2. Add the three numbers. The sum is _____

3. Subtract 1000. The new number is _____

4. Add 46. The new number is _____

5. Cross out any zeros. The treasure is waiting in Room Number _____

Surprise! The treasure was hidden in the students' own classroom. When the teams got back, their teacher had treasure bags with party treats for everyone.

The Case of the Treasure Hunt
Teacher's Guide

The End-of-the-Year Party (p. 54)

Introduce the scenario of the boys helping their teacher plan a class party on p. 54. Discuss how a treasure hunt works. If the students have completed "The Case of the Missing Mascot," they will be familiar with this type of activity.

Solving the First Clue (p. 55)

The students will need to use some resource to locate the information needed to solve this clue. You may want to brainstorm possible sources with them. Have them use the clues on p. 55 as guidelines for figuring out the answer. It's best to start with a list of presidents, then narrow them down using the other clues.

Answer: Ulysses S. Grant

Cracking Clue 2's Cryptic Message (p. 56)

Before students begin work on the cryptogram puzzle on p. 56, you may want to review the cryptograms they solved in the section called "Shirley's Tests for New Members" (pp. 7–15).

Answer: It's hidden in the nurse's office, on her desk.

Seeking Out Other Students (p. 57)

Direct students to solve the Special Class Puzzle on p. 57. Point out to them that because each girl has two special classes, they cannot fill in "no" answers horizontally until they have two "yes" answers for a particular girl.

Answers: Shirley Sharp has physical education at 9 a.m. and art at 10:45 a.m.; Betty Bright has physical education at 9:30 a.m. and music at 9 a.m.; Sara

Sharp has physical education at 2 p.m. and art at 1 p.m.; Cathy Quest has physical education at 10 a.m. and music at 9:45 a.m.; The person who has art class at 10:45 a.m. is Shirley Sharp. She has the next clue.

Unscrambling Clue 4 (p. 58)

Review the meaning of an anagram puzzle with the students before they begin the puzzle on p. 58 (See "Shirley's Tests for New Members" section, pp. 7–15).

Answer: The playground is where clue number five is hidden. It is taped under the seat of the middle swing.

Visiting Classrooms (p. 59)

The clue at the playground tells the students that the next clue is in Michael's desk, but they must first figure out to which class Michael belongs. Introduce the logic puzzle on p. 59 and have student's solve it to find Michael's teacher and grade. (Note: The difficulty level of this puzzle is greater than the previous logic puzzles in this book.)

Answers: Gabriel—Ms. Springer, Grade 3; Ling—Ms. Gonzales, Grade 3; Justin—Ms. Steinbach, Grade 4; Michael—Ms. Hawes, Grade 3; Luke—Mr. Delaney, Grade 5; Julia—Ms. Dorn, Grade 4; Kyle—Mr. Dresdow, Grade 4; Dong Mei—Ms. Strum, Grade 5; Pedro—Mr. Sing, Grade 5; Michael is in Ms. Hawes' class.

Finally, The Treasure! (p. 60)

Direct the students to solve the number puzzle on p. 60. You may want to allow some students to use a calculator.

Answers: 1a.) 24; 1b.) 665; 1c.) 765; 2.) 1454; 3.) 454; 4.) 500; 5.) 5; The treasure is in Room 5.

About the Authors

Sharon Eckert and Judy Leimbach have been friends and colleagues since they began working together in 1975 on the first and second multigrade team at Briar Glen School in Community Consolidated School District 89 in Glen Ellyn, IL. In 1980, Judy changed to a new teaching position, becoming the school's Challenge Teacher in District 89's new gifted program. In this position, she worked with gifted students in grades 1–5.

Judy's first book, *Primarily Logic*, was the result of developing her own materials for her classes when few were available for young students. She continued to write materials for use in gifted programs and also for regular classroom teachers to use in meeting the needs of their advanced students. Judy has collaborated with colleagues on 11 of her 16 books. Prior to working on this book, Sharon Eckert and Judy Leimbach coauthored *Math Extension Units for Grades 2–3*, *Primarily Math*, *Primarily Literature*, *Primary Book Reporter*, and *Detective Club*.

Sharon has devoted her teaching career to the education of primary students. She has taught kindergarten through third grade; however, second grade is her favorite, and she chose to teach at that level for 30 years. During her years of service in District 89, Sharon has served on district curriculum committees in language arts, math, and social studies; district committees for report cards, textbook adoptions, and teacher in-service; and numerous building committees. Her interest in photography has led her to record various events and social functions throughout the district. Judy calls her the "District Historian."

After retirement, Judy supervised student teachers at Wheaton College and did consulting in gifted education, presenting workshops in various parts of the country. She now enjoys working in various volunteer activities, traveling with her husband, and getting together with friends for book club, Bible study groups, and RODEO club (Real Old Dames Eating Out!).

Sharon earned her bachelor's degree in education and master's degree in education from Illinois State University. Judy received her bachelor's degree in education from Ball State University and her master's degree in instructional strategies in gifted education from National Louis University.

Common Core State Standards Alignment Sheet

Grade Level	Common Core State Standards in ELA-Literacy
Grade 2	RF.2.3 Know and apply grade-level phonics and word analysis skills in decoding words
	RF.2.4 Read with sufficient accuracy and fluency to support comprehension.
Grade 3	RF.3.3 Know and apply grade-level phonics and word analysis skills in decoding words
	RF.3.4 Read with sufficient accuracy and fluency to support comprehension.
Grade 4	RF.4.3 Know and apply grade-level phonics and word analysis skills in decoding words
	RF.4.4 Read with sufficient accuracy and fluency to support comprehension.

Printed in the United States
by Baker & Taylor Publisher Services